Ninety Love Octaves

Legas

Pueti D'Arba Sicula Series

Volume VII

Series Editor: Gaetano Cipolla

Other Volumes Published in this Series:

Volume 1
Vincenzo Ancona, *Malidittu la lingua/Damned Language*, edited by Anna Chairetakis and Joseph Sciorra, translated into English by Gaetano Cipolla, 1990;

Volume II
The Poetry of Nino Martoglio, edited, introduced and translated by Gaetano Cipolla, 1993;

Volume III
Giovanni Meli, *Moral Fables and Other Poems*, edited, introduced and translated by Gaetano Cipolla, 1995;

Volume IV
Antonino Provenzano, *Vinissi/I'd Love to Come...*, edited and translated by Gaetano Cipolla, 1995;

Volume V
Sicilian Erotica, edited and translated by Gaetano Cipolla, introduction by Justin Vitiello, 1997.

Volume VI
Giovanni Meli, *Don Chisciotti and Sanciu Panza*, edited, introduced and translated by Gaetano Cipolla, 2003.

Antonio Veneziano

Ninety Love Octaves

**Edited, introduced, and translated
into English Verse**

by Gaetano Cipolla

LEGAS

Library of Congress Cataloging-in-Publication Data

Veneziano, Antonio, 1543-1593.
  [Ottave. English & Italian]
  Ninety love octaves / Antonio Veneziano ; edited, introduced, and translated into English verse by Gaetano Cipolla.
      p. cm. — (Pueti d'Arba Sicula ; v. 7)
  English with original Italian (Sicilian) text of poems.
  Includes bibliographical references.
  ISBN 1-881901-56-4 (pbk.)
  I. Cipolla, Gaetano, 1937- II. Title.
  PQ4664.V314O813 2006
  851'.4—dc22

                               2006028275

Acknowledgements
The publisher is grateful to Arba Sicula for a generous grant that in part made the publication of this book possible.

Printed in Canada

For information and for orders, write to:

Legas

P.O. Box 149
Mineola, New York
11501, USA

3 Wood Aster Bay
Ottawa, Ontario
Canada K2R1D3

Legaspublishing.com

To my mother,
one octave, almost,
for each
of her 92 years of age.

Table of Contents

CELIA/CELIA

LIBRU II DI CANZUNI AMURUSI SICILIANI/II BOOK OF SICILIAN LOVE SONGS

PROVERBII/PROVERBS

Introduction

My interest in Antonio Veneziano was sparked by the poet's attitudes toward the Sicilian language and his insistence on using that language in his work. He claimed that he could have written in other languages but if he did so he would have behaved like a parrot that does not have a language of its own and imitates the language it hears. Thus Veneziano seemed to me a staunch defender of the native idiom against the spreading influence of Tuscan in Sicily. He represents a point in history when in fact the predominance of Tuscan as the literary language of Italy was becoming an accepted fact. As Franco Lo Piparo showed in his recreation of the linguistic history of Sicilian, the middle of the 16th century saw Tuscan finally affirm itself as the literary and bureaucratic language of Sicily, even though Sicilian was the only language spoken by the populace.[1] But for written documents Tuscan overcame Sicilian.

Antonio Veneziano made a conscious choice, not only because he was aware that writing in one's native language was an essential element in the ability of the poet to express his innermost thoughts and ideas, but also because he wanted give luster to the language of Sicily which had been the first Italic poetic idiom in the early part of the thirteenth century. His letter of dedication which served as a preface to his first volume of canzuni entitled *Celia* is an important statement in defense of his choice of language but also a precious document to understand the poet's attitude toward poetry and his work. It behooves us to read a portion of it:

> "Perhaps the world expects different fruits from my wit, but in what language could I begin if not with the language that I learned first and suckled with my milk? [...] It would certainly be odd if Homer who was Greek and wrote in Greek, Horace who lived where Latin was spoken and wrote in Latin, Petrarch who was Tuscan and wrote in Tuscan, if I who am Sicilian did not find it more appropriate to write in Sicilian. And if Plautus had the high grace to imitate the first Sicilian comic playwright Epicharmus, and Virgil was happy to bring back the *Idylls* of Theocritus who was also Sicilian, I who am Sicilian

11

have to become a parrot mouthing the language of others? Oh Tuscan is more widely understood and is more common! That is true in Italy, not on Sicily, nor is it more understood by Sicilian women whom the majority of poets try to please and serve. What was more miraculous, Phidias who made a Minerva in ivory or a horse of stone? Poetry does not reside in the idiom: it resides in the vein, in the spirit and in the thoughts: although I, thanks be to God, know how to write in other languages, for now it pleased me to show myself with my own face. When I want to wear a mask I will show that I too can play my part well, as anybody else can play theirs. And if I wanted to satisfy myself more, I would have written many odes and epigrams. But let everyone realize that a great emotion cannot be better expressed than in the mother's language. Thus we can see as when one is prey to wrath or overly cheerful he begins immediately to speak his native tongue even though he may be well versed in other languages." (my translation). [2]

Thus his use of Sicilian was in itself an act of rebellion against the ever widening sphere of use of Tuscan, a way of swimming upstream against the strong current of the Tuscan idiom, at the same time as it was an affirmation of the validity of Sicilian as a tool of poetic expression. In doing this, of course, he was linking his work to the great Sicilian School of poetry which flourished under the Emperor Frederick II, when Sicilian was the dominant language of poetry for a hundred years. As Dante said, Sicilians were the first and everything written before his time was Sicilian. [3]

Veneziano was true to his conviction and wrote primarily in Sicilian and the great majority of his compositions are "Canzuni", that is, eight lines of hendecasyllables with alternating rhyme, which is the most characteristic of the Sicilian poetic compositions from which the sonnet emerged in Sicily by adding six more lines. A measure of his great devotion to the language of his home can be seen when, contrary to what probably was becoming a *de facto* custom among literate people, instead of using Tuscanized Sicilian, he proclaimed his innocence against the accusation of murder brought against him and his brothers, in Sicilian. In another case where he was accused of acts of violence against a herd of sheep that was grazing on his land, Veneziano presented his written defense in Sicilian, while his accuser wrote in siculo-tuscan and the Judge rendered his verdict in Latin. Veneziano, perhaps to prove that he could also write in Italian and Latin, wrote a "Fonte Pretorio: Discorso sopra le statue della fontana pretoria di Palermo," which is a description of the so-called "Funtana da vriogna," (the Fountain of Shame on account of all its naked statues) that was placed in the square before the Palermo Town Hall, and he was asked to write the inscription on the tomb of William II that can still be read today in the Monreale Cathedral.

But this of course, is not the only reason for wanting to celebrate the work of Veneziano. He stands as the universally acclaimed prince of Sicilian Renaissance poetry whose influence and importance is felt for many centuries after his death. He was so admired not only by the literati but by the Sicilian people that many works with which he had absolutely nothing to do have been ascribed to him.

Antonello Veneziano was born in Monreale on the 7 of January of 1543. His father, Antonio Veneziano, had married three wives and had children from all three. Antonello, (that was his original name until he changed it to Antonio presumably after his father's death) was the third of the seven children his father had with the last wife Allegranza Azzolino. His father's last name may have been Vallone and "Veneziano" may have been simply the identification of his birth place. He was a well educated man of means and political connections to the Farnese family which governed the City of Monreale at the time. As Vicar of Cardinal Farnese, the Magnifico Antonio Veneziano held a position of power in Monreale. His brother Antonino was *arcidiacono* and was placed in charge of the young Antonello when his father passed away when he was barely four years old. When Antonio was twelve years old he entered the college of the Society of Jesus in Palermo. Having completed his study of grammar in Palermo, he went on to the college of Messina which was the only one on the island that offered specialized courses in the humanities, literature, rethorics, Greek and Hebrew and must have excelled because he was sent to Rome together with three other Sicilian students to complete his preparation with the famous philosopher Francesco Toleto, who was to become a cardinal. Antonio remained in Rome for three years, but his vocation must not have been the strongest for shortly after the death of his uncle Antonino, he left the Society of Jesus in good terms, it seems, and with the blessing of his superiors. The decision to leave the order may have been aided by a provision in his uncle's will. Antonio was to receive from his two brothers a decent suit of clothing while he remained in the Society of Jesus, but if for whatever reason he decided to leave the order, he was to inherit a share equal to that of his brothers.

Judging by the behavior that followed his separation from the Order, Antonio provided ample evidence that he was not made for the life of seclusion and study that characterizes the Jesuits. In 1564 he was accused of murdering Antonio Polizzi together with his brothers Nicolò and Giovanni. The three were arrested and spent some time in jail. They were freed, but a few months afterward all three were banned from the City of Monreale for four years. Apparently, Antonio was not involved in the murder, but his brothers readily admitted to having taken part in the hunt for Polizzi who was a known felon hunted by the officers of the Court. Eventually Antonio was allowed to reenter the city, thanks to the intercession of the Count of Vicari with the Viceroy, the Marquis of Pescara. Needless to say, this was not the first, nor the last time that Veneziano had dealings with the courts and with jail. In the thirty years from 1563 to 1593, Antonio was in and out of jail innumerable times, literally spending the best years of his life behind bars. In 1573, for example, he was again in prison for having kidnapped (willingly, it seems) a young maid from her mistress, sister Eufrigenia Diana, a Dominican nun. The accuser also alleged that he had stolen a sum of money along with Franceschella Porretta. It is not known how Antonio managed to settle this affair, but he was embroiled in a dispute about property with his brothers and with his own mother who eventually disowned him as a disobedient son. Not long after his mother's death in 1574, Antonio, perhaps out of a desire to show that he was not interested so much in material things, donated his inheritance rights to Eufemia de Calogero, his sister Vincenza's daughter, in whose house he had been staying while banned from Monreale. The donation carried an unusual clause: it stipulated that the niece could neither get married nor become a nun, remaining always chaste and honest on pain of losing the inheritance. The nature of the donation invites speculation with some critics such as Gaetano Millunzi,[4] believing that Veneziano had absolutely no interests in the niece, who was about the same age as he was, other than her Christian education and upbringing; others, like

Leonardo Sciascia,[5] suggest that behind the niece's identity stands the woman who was to inspire most of his love poems and whose name, Celia, is used as the title of the first volume of *canzuni*. The other women who were the object of Veneziano's attention are readily recognizable. Francisca is Franceschella Porretta and Isabella is Isabella La Turri, but no one has identified Celia. The need for keeping the identity of Celia absolutely secret has nothing to do with the medieval notion that once a love becomes of public knowledge it dies. It had to do with the shame and blame that would be theirs if a love relationship between uncle and niece were made public.

Another event that landed Veneziano in jail was not due to his sharp tongue or to his violent and arrogant nature. It was an act of piracy for which he cannot be held responsible. The ship on which Veneziano was traveling was part of a convoy that escorted Don Carlos of Aragon from Palermo to Spain to be named Governor of Milan in exchange for his position as President of the Kingdom of Sicily. The ships had left Palermo on the 25 of April 1578 and were near the island of Capri when they were spotted by a fleet of Algerian pirates. The lead ship was able to escape but the ship that was trailing behind was captured by the pirates. The vessel was boarded and after fierce resistance, the Sicilians were subdued by the pirates who proceeded to take all prisoners to Algiers to await ransom.

When Veneziano arrived in Algiers, another distinguished prisoner had been living in jail for three years. His name was Miguel de Cervantes. The author of the *Don Quijote de la Mancha* and the Sicilian poet met and the two developed a relationship of mutual admiration. Cervantes wrote a long poem (twelve octaves) after he read Veneziano's *Celia* in which he praised the poems as worthy of paradise. The letter that accompanied the poem is signed "En Argel, los seis de Noviembre 1579. De V.M. verdadero amigo y servidor, Miguel de Cerbantes." For his part Veneziano responded with a poem, that Sciascia termed "incredibilmente brutta" [6]. The two remained in Algiers for about two years, until they were ransomed. Cervantes left toward Spain on the 24 of October 1580 and Veneziano, whose ransom was probably paid by a collection from among his friends, was already in Monreale on the 28 of November of the same year.

It was not long before he had to appear before a tribunal to answer a claim against him for 450 ounces from his sisters Maria and Virginia, both nuns. He was also involved in a violent altercation with the owner of a herd of sheep who he claimed allowed the animals to feed on his pastures illegally. Together with two other men, Veneziano burst into the corral where 950 sheep were kept and ordered his men to "kill as many sheep as you can for these bastards have ruined me!" The men proceeded to scatter the herd and 450 of the 950 were dispersed in the dark and could not be recovered. In the ensuing trial the owner of the herd maintained that the sheep grazed on the land with Veneziano's permission. He had no signed documents, however. And it is difficult to know who was right in the case.

I will mention one final episode of Veneziano's never ending troubles with the law and with the authorities. Veneziano was arrested and tortured in 1588 under suspicion of having penned a *Pasquinade* against the Viceroy don Diego Enriques de Guzmán Count of Alba. Having resisted seven turns of the cord, Veneziano was eventually released. But apparently the Count of Alba remembered Veneziano when two years later another cartoon that depicted him as a "jettatore", (a bringer of bad luck) was posted in town. The poet was suspected of being the culprit and thrown into jail in the fortress of Castellammare del Golfo. It is not clear whether Veneziano spent three years in jail for an insulting cartoon. There is evidence that he was out of jail in 1591 and 1592. But as he seemed unable to control his wit, it's likely that he committed a similar offense against the new viceroy, the Count of Olivares and ended up in jail again. Vincenzo Di Giovanni in his *Palermo restaurato* wrote that Veneziano was responsible for writing another offensive poster and that he was betrayed by his friends. Sciascia cites an octave, attributed to Veneziano, that speaks of life in prison and betrayal that goes as follows:

Amici, amici, quadari, quadari,
Facitimi quadari di liscia,
Ca tutti quanti mi vogghiu squadari
Li robbi di la Vicaria.
Curriti, curriti, mastri pittinari
Purtati tutti pettini pri mia;

E s"un c'è corna, faciti sirrari
Li corna a chiddi chi 'nfussaru a mia.

My friends, my friends, cauldrons and cauldrons bring,
many a cauldron full of lye prepare
for me because I want to wash away
the filthy clothes soiled in the Vicaria;
Come running all of you, master comb makers,
Bring all the combs you have in stock for me
And if you cannot find horns readily,
Go saw the horns off those who buried me.

Whether or not this is true, one thing is certain: Antonio Veneziano was again imprisoned in the fortress of Castellammare and on the 19 of August 1593, when there was a fire and an explosion of the munitions held in the fortress, he was buried under the rubble, together with a number of other prisoners, ending his turbulent and troubled existence.

It is difficult to reconcile the man and the poet. Leonardo Sciascia painted a terrible picture of the man in his brief sketch of the poet. Veneziano was according to him: "Violent, sensual, prodigal, full of debts (and of the French disease, according to a later biographer of his, inconstant in familiar feelings and in love, absolutely devoid of respect for institutions and for the men that represented them)…: this was Antonio Veneziano." [7]

That Veneziano had a terrible reputation as an arrogant, litigious man who was not too squeamish to use his ever ready sword is readily conceded by most critics. But if you try to get a picture of the man from his poetry alone, you would have a difficult time reconciling the man with the poet. His poetry is not autobiographical, as was noted by Luigi Natoli in a study of the poet from Monreale:

"It would be useless to try to find the man in the writer: In Veneziano there is only the indifferent artist who does not care to reveal himself to us. His life, his feelings are something extraneous to his art or they enter into it by accident not as a source of inspiration. Thus in his works in verse or in prose we cannot find the citizen: he is an artist in the true sense of the word for whom the form is all."[8]

Nevertheless, as Contini shows, the true biography is the one that emerges from a study of his poetry. It is there, in the eight hundred plus *canzuni* that comprise the bulk of his poetic production, not to mention the many hundreds more that were attributed to him, that he expressed his wit, his cleverness and his artistic persona. He lives more in the reputation that emerges from his *canzuni* than from the time-bound accidents of his life. And in his reputation as a poet, there is no one in the Sicilian landscape that comes close to him. Vincenzo Di Giovanni wrote about him in hyperbolic praise:

> "He was the best in our country: he possessed a sharp and keen mind, he was extremely and learned, his style was heroic and sublime and he excelled in performing deed. His canzuni were so praiseworthy that everything beautiful was measured against him and were of such sort that every professor of poetry, even in Italy, wished to have Veneziano's *canzuni* to use his conceits in their own poetry. Among our poets a good style was one that came close to his." [9] (My translation)

Not only was he considered by poets and critics of his time the meter by which to measure great poetry, his reputation was even higher among the people of Sicily. Indeed, it is astonishing that he enjoyed such a reputation considering the relatively few printed volumes of his work. His reputation consolidated itself primarily through the oral transmission of his texts, which explains why so many poems are erroneously attributed to him. A measure of the stature of Veneziano among the populace can be seen in Giuseppe Pitrè's study entitled "Antonio Veneziano nella leggenda popolare siciliana".[10] Pitrè explained that when a person becomes famous, either for deeds of valor or for exceptional virtues or vices, he is absorbed intensely by the imagination of his contemporaries and of those that come afterwards. Such a mythicizing must have occurred with the figure of Veneziano. Pitrè stated categorically that "as a poet he was undoubtedly the strongest and the most facile according to the tradition. Nobody could stand up against him while alive and nobody could overcome him when he was dead. Our people attribute to Veneziano whatever literary and beautiful quality it has been able to discover in the songs." [11]

Let us now look at Veneziano's style and at the language that he used. Writing in the second half of the 16th century, when the

Petrarchism that was the dominant mode of expression in Italy and in all of Europe was evolving into Mannerism, Veneziano who has been called "the Sicilian Petrarch", was perhaps more correctly identified as a "Petrarchist with a manneristic line," as did Prof. Nicolò Mineo.[12] As reductive as such classification are, Prof. Mineo's characterization can be accepted as accurate, but a few distinctions must be made to further define Veneziano's style. It is true that Veneziano used the themes and the psychological situations of Petrarch's *Canzoniere*, but it is also true that much of his repertory was derived from the Sicilian folkloric and popular tradition. At the same time, however, the use of popular themes and folk motifs does not mean that Veneziano's style is popular. For the choice of language and for the style of his verse the poetry of *Celia* remains "nelle stesse zone alte del sistema letterario: poesia seria e non comica," as Franco Brevini put it.[13] Veneziano adopted a language that was an illustrious Sicilian that refrains from using every day expressions, or words that could be deemed as reproducing street jargon. The language of the *canzuni* in *Celia* remains sublime, that is, highly literary without ever descending, as Meli allowed himself to do occasionally, to use words and expressions straight out of the mouth of the people. His language was meant as an affirmation of the validity of an illustrious Sicilian that could be put side by side with Tuscan without being considered inferior. For this reason, he maintained a restrictive and controlled attitude toward his choice of words. This is an operation that was akin to what Petrarch himself did when writing the *Canzoniere*. Unlike Dante who adopted a much freer and much more inclusive attitude, Petrarch was very selective in his use of words, reducing them to the barest essential to guarantee their survival as much as possible. Contini spoke of this as an attempt to remove the temporality of words and relegate them to a timeless zone. Veneziano attempts perhaps something similar by refraining from the colloquial, shunning the spoken idiom and the idiomatic expressions of his day in favor of a higher level of language that Dante would have called "aulico". It has been noted also that while the language he used was Sicilian, the underlying syntactical structure was Tuscan.

The second part of Mineo's characterization of Veneziano's style needs to be addressed as well. I am referring to his "Manneristic line". Petrarch's predilections for oxymora, antithesis, repetitions and conceits, that is, all the external elements of his style which he himself sometimes expanded and exaggerated, slipping into what is known as Mannerism, becomes the bases for many of Veneziano's *canzuni*. He often makes use of a clever remark, of an ingenious situation, of an extended metaphor on which to construct a *canzuna*. What the Spaniards called "agudeza," that is, a sharp intuition, a witty "trovata" often constitutes the point of departure for an octave. No doubt the fact that Mannerism, which was so popular in Spain, where it was known as *Gongorismo* after its major exponent Luis Gongora, had to have some influence on Sicily where Spanish culture was certainly felt and on Veneziano himself.

Another point of distinction between Petrarch and Veneziano is in the fact that the *Canzoniere* was painstakingly constructed according to a master design, a need for unity that somehow reflected individual moments in the life story of its persona. There are 366 poems in the *Canzoniere* mimicking the days of the year, forming a circular motion that has neither beginning nor end, the first poem sees the poet at the same stage of development as the last, but in the *Celia*, there is no discernible attempt at unity, no coherent design.

Nevertheless, Antonio Veneziano represents the highest point of Sicilian Renaissance poetry and is to be considered the initiator of the Sicilian dialect tradition out of which would come great poets such as Giovanni Meli, Domenico Tempio, Nino Martoglio, Alessio di Giovanni, Santo Calì, Ignazio Buttitta, Salvatore Camilleri, Salvatore Di Marco and Nino De Vita.

***

A word about the Veneziano opus as described by Gaetana Maria Rinaldi who has embarked on the arduous task of sifting through the manuscripts, trying to make sense of the complex and often unreliable way with which the poems have been published. While there are numerous manuscripts that attribute many poems to Veneziano that he certainly did not write, Rinaldi has been able to identify a manuscript that is the most reliable and authoritative which contains 289 canzuni under the title of *Celia*, which is regarded as the major *canzoniere* of the poet, 313 *canzuni* under the title of *Libru secundu di canzuni amurusi siciliani*; 42 *Canzuni di sdegnu* (Songs of Contempt). In addition, the manuscript, which is known as XI.B.6, contains 33 *canzuni spirituali* and 100 more without titles. These are all the poems that are surely Veneziano's. In addition, he wrote a trilogy entitled "Puttanismu," "Arangeida" and "Cornaria," obviously in the satiric mode, as well as two lamentations called "Nenia" and "Agonia".[14]

Hundreds of poems more have been attributed to Veneziano, as well as a collection of *Proverbii*, which were praised by Giuseppe Pitrè, whose authorship has been questioned by modern scholarship. We have chosen to include a few of these proverbs which people have associated with Veneziano for centuries. They are part of the persona of Veneziano that lived in the consciousness of the Sicilian people and were transmitted from generation to generation through a rich oral tradition. As I said earlier, Veneziano's fame and poetry owe much to the oral tradition.

The choice of the ninety octaves contained in this volume was not made with any systematic design in mind. There was no attempt to construct a line of development, only to give as wide a sampling to let the readers see the breadth and the scope of Veneziano's poetry. To avoid conflicting numbers, we have assigned no numbers to the ninety poems, preferring to use the first line as the title of the *canzuna*. Since a critical edition has yet to be published, this seemed the least problematic.

The translation tries to be as close to the original as possible, using a iambic pentameter with the final couplet of each octave rhymed, whenever possible. Trying to follow the Sicilian alternating rhyming scheme would have imposed far too many compromises with the meaning and rhythm of the line.

Notes

1. Franco Lo Piparo, "Sicilia Linguistica," in *Le Regioni dall'Unità a oggi, La Sicilia*, Torino: Giulio Einaudi Editore, 1987.

2. Lo Piparo, p. 741

3. Dante Alighieri, *De Vulgari Eloquentia*, ed. and trans by Steve Botterill, Cambridge University Press, 1996, p. 29.

4. Gaetano Millunzi, *Del sole, della luna dello sguardo: Vita e Opere di A. Veneziano*, Ed. Novecento, Palermo, 1994.

5. For the biographical information I am relying on Sciascia's sketch, published in *Antonio Veneziano: Ottave*, a cura di Leonardo Sciascia, Gaetana Maria Rinaldi, Pietro Mazzamuto, Edizione Comune di Monreale, 1990.

6. See Sciascia, op. cit. p. 26.

7. See Sciascia, op. cit. p. 16.

8. "Antonio Veneziano," in *Prosa e prosatori siciliani del secolo XVI*, Ed. Remo Sandron, Palermo 1904, p.101.

9. As quoted by L. Sciascia, op. cit., p. 35.

10. in *Archivio Storico Siciliano* a. XIX Ed. Lo Statuto, Palermo 1894.

11. as quoted by Salvatore Di Marco in "Riflessi dell'opera di A. Veneziano nella poesia dialettale siciliana," in *Antonio Veneziano*: Atti del convegno a cura di Salvatore di Marco, Edizioni: Provincia regionale di Palermo, 2000, p. 50.

12. "La poesia dialettale siciliana sino al primo Ottocento," in *Letteratura dialettale preunitaria*, vol. II p. 1075.

13. Franco Brevini, "Petrarchismo e antipetrarchismo in dialetto," in *Antonio Veneziano*: Atti del convegno a cura di Salvatore di Marco, Edizioni: Provincia regionale di Palermo, 2000, p 40.

14. See Rinaldi's study "L'edizione delle rime siciliane di A. Veneziano," in *Antonio Veneziano*: Atti del convegno a cura di Salvatore di Marco, Edizioni: Provincia regionale di Palermo, 2000.

Bibliography

Antonio Biondolillo, "Un celebre poeta del Cinquecento in Sicilia: A. Veneziano," in *Saggi e Ricerche*, Studio Eitoriale Mderno, Catania 1926.

Franco Brevini, "etrarchismo e anti-petrarchismo in dialetto," *Antonio Veneziano* in Atti del convegno a cura di Salvatore di Marco, Edizioni: Provincia regionale di Palermo, 2000.

Vincenzo Di Giovanni, *Palermo restaurato*, a cura di G. Di Marzio Palermo, 1872.

Salvatore Di Marco, "Riflessi dell'opera di A. Veneziano nella poesia dialettale siciliana," in *Antonio Veneziano*: Atti del convegno a cura di Salvatore di Marco, Edizioni: Provincia regionale di Palermo, 2000.

V. Epifanio, *La Celia di A. Veneziano*, Palermo, 1901.

Aldo Gerbino, "Millunzi storico, critico e il Veneziano," in *Antonio Veneziano*: Atti del convegno a cura di Salvatore di Marco, Edizioni: Provincia regionale di Palermo, 2000.

Pino Giacopelli, "Antonio Veneziano e il suo tempo a Monreale," in Antonio Veneziano: Atti del convegno a cura di Salvatore di Marco, Edizioni: Provincia regionale di Palermo, 2000.

Sebastiano Grasso, "Per una canzuna di A. Veneziano," in *Antonio Veneziano*: Atti del convegno a cura di Salvatore di Marco, Edizioni: Provincia regionale di Palermo, 2000.

Isidoro La Lumia, "Antonio Veneziano o un cinquecentista di Sicilia," in *Nuova Antologia*, XV, 1879.

Franco Lo Piparo, "Sicilia Linguistica," in *Le Regioni dall'Unità a oggi, La Sicilia*, Torino: Giulio Einaudi Editore, 1987.

G.E. Ortolani, *Biografia degli uomini illustri della Sicilia*, Napoli, 1818.

Gaetano Millunzi, *Del sole, della luna dello sguardo: Vita e Opere di A. Veneziano*, Ed. Novecento, Palermo, 1994.

—— "Antonio Veneziano," in "Archivio Storio Siciliano", Nuova Serie, XIX 1894.

Giuseppe Pitrè, "Antonio Veneziano nella leggenda popolare siciliana," in *Archivio Storico Siciliano*, Nuova serie, XIX, 1894.

—— *Studi di poesia popolare*, Palermo, 1876.

Luigi Natoli, Prosa *e prosatori siciliani del secolo XVI*, Palermo, 1904.

—— *Musa Siciliana*, Casa Editrice R. Caddeo, Milano 1922.

Pietro Mazzamuto, "Antonio Veneziano nella cultura del suo tempo," in *Storia della Sicilia*, Palermo-Napoli, 1980 Vol IV.

Nicolò Mineo, "La poesia dialettale siciliana sino al primo Ottocento," in *Letteratura dialettale preunitaria*, vol II.

Gaetana Maria Rinaldi, "Repertorio delle *canzuni* siciliane nei secoli XVI-XVII," in *Bollettino del Centro Studi Filologici e Linguistici Siciliani*, 18, 1995.

—— "L'edizione delle rime siciliane di A. Veneziano," in *Antonio Veneziano*: Atti del convegno a cura di Salvatore di Marco, Edizioni: Provincia regionale di Palermo, 2000.

Antonio Veneziano, Atti del convegno a cura di Salvatore di Marco, Edizioni: Provincia Regionale di Palermo, 2000.

Antonio Veneziano: Ottave, a cura di Leonardo Sciascia, Gaetana Maria Rinaldi, Pietro Mazzamuto, Edizione Comune di Monreale, 1990.

S. Vento, *Il culto del Petrarca in Sicilia dal Veneziano al Meli*, Firenze, 1931.

Rita Verdirame, "Modelli e moduli della lirica d'amore nelle ottave di A. Veneziano," in *Antonio Veneziano*: Atti del convegno a cura di Salvatore di Marco, Edizioni: Provincia regionale di Palermo, 2000.

Celia

Celia

IN OGNI LOCU M'IMAGINU E CRIJU

In ogni locu m'imaginu e criju
per miu confortu ritrovarci a tia:
ma quandu, ohimè, m'addugnu poi e m'avviju,
cosa non trovu chi comu tia sia.
Perchì, si per l'ardenti e gran disiju
ccà e ddà mi fingiu chiddu chi vurria,
sai chi su li cosi chi viju?
Figura tua di terra e tu la dia.

'MMATULA A DARMI MORTI TI LAMBICHI

'Mmatula a darmi morti ti lambichi,
e d'ogni modu chi poi e sai, m'aucidi,
chi tantu chiù grann'almu mi nutrichi,
quantu chiù a grann'imprisa mi disfidi;
Si tuttu mi pizzii e mi smuddichi,
cridimi, beni miu, cridimi, cridi,
ch'in tanti specchi, muddichi muddichi,
vidirai lu to aspettu, e la mia fidi.

I FANTASIZE AND THEN CONVINCE MYSELF

I fantasize and then convince myself
to my relief, I see you everywhere,
but when, alas, I realize and look
I can't find anyone that is like you.
For through the ardent yearning for your face
I make believe I see you here and there,
in truth, do you know what all these things are?
earth images of you and you their star.

NO MATTER HOW YOU STRAIN TO GIVE ME DEATH

No matter how you strain to give me death
and injure me in every way you know,
you will give only boldness to my courage,
challenging me to fight a greater battle.
If you make crumbs of me, tear me to bits,
believe me, my beloved, do believe,
that you will find in every tiny piece
my faith and a reflection of your own face.

CU CHIDDI SOI MODUZZI SAPURITI

Cu chiddi soi moduzzi sapuriti
mi spiau un ghiornu cui era lu miu dardu.
"Guardatimi intra l'occhi e vidiriti
-ci diss'iu - chi dda pari per cui ardu!"
-Guardau, si vitti e risi e - chi criditi? –
-suggiunsi un tiru chiù beddu e gagghiardu:
- "Guarda chi latru gintili chi siti,
chi rubati li genti cu lu sguardu!".

DI POI CHI PERSI, NÉ SPERU CHIÙ AVIRI

Di poi chi persi, né speru chiù aviri
Chidda, per cui campava consolatu,
Cori, chi senti? Peni. Occhiu, chi miri?
Tenebri. Auricchia, ch'audi? Chiantu e urlatu.
Vucca, chi gusti? Tossicu e suspiri.
Chi prov'anima? Guai. Tu, xhiatu? Patu.
E comu siti vivi a sti martiri?
Cori, occhiu, auricchia, vucca, anima e xhiatu?

WITH HER SWEET CHARMING WAYS SHE ASKED ONE DAY

With her sweet, charming ways she asked one day
whose arrow had pierced through my heart. I said,
"Look in my eyes, and you will see the one
for whom I burn." She looked and saw herself
and smiled. And then—Would you believe her
                                    gall?—
a sweeter and more powerful attack
she launched "You see, you are a gentle crook!
You steal incautious people as you look!"

SINCE I HAVE LOST THE ONE FOR WHOM I LIVED

Since I have lost the one for whom in bliss
I lived, and have no hope to ever get her back,
what do you feel, heart? Pain. What see you, eyes?
Darkness. What hear you, ears? Just screams and cries.
What do you taste, mouth? Poison and great sighs.
What do you feel, soul? Woes. You, breath? Distress.
How come these woes have not yet caused you death,
My heart, eyes, ears, my mouth, my soul, and breath?

DI L' OCCHI TOI LU STILI POTTI TANTU

Di l' occhi toi lu stili potti tantu
chi in lagrimi squagghiau la carni mia,
si tornava a guardarmi un autru tantu
comu vapuri e l'airu m'attraia.
O, s'iu chicassi mai tant'autu quantu
nevula d'acqua facissi di mia,
non chioggia d'oru, ma chioggia di chiantu
dintra l'amata tuttu trasiria!

OH, SI SPINTA DI COLLERA E DI STIZZA

Oh, si spinta di collera e di stizza
cu li manuzzi toi mi maltrattassi,
ed iu - chi non sia mai! - fussi sulfizza,
per puru istintu chi ti muzzicassi,
quantu si saziria la tua ferizza
supra di mia, s'a posta tua sburrassi,
e quanta sarria poi la mia allegrizza
chi cu la morti mia ti risanassi!

THE SUN OUT OF YOUR EYES WAS OF SUCH MIGHT

The sun out of your eyes was of such might
it melted my poor flesh to streams of tears
and if it gazed on me a little more,
it would have turned me into rising vapor.
O if I ever rose to such a height
that I became a water-laden cloud,
a rain of tears I'd be, not a gold shower,
and I would enter my beloved tower.*

IF OVERCOME WITH ANGER AND PERTURBED

If overcome with anger and perturbed
you should maltreat me with your own sweet hands
and — God forbid!—I were a scorpion,
and acting on pure instinct I bit you,
as you went on to sate your cruelty,
venting your wrath on me to please yourself,
how truly wondrous would be my delight
if with my death I healed you from my bite.**

---

* The poet is referring to the myth of Danae whose father hid her away in a tower to protect her from Zeus' love attentions. The plan, of course, did not work because Zeus changed himself into a shower of gold and impregnated Danae anyway.

** Note. It was a popular belief that a scorpion's bite could be cured only after the death of the scorpion.

Nasci in Sardigna un'erva, anzi un venenu,
chi, cui ndi gusta, di li risa mori:
né antitodi ci ponnu di Galenu,
né d'Esculapiu incantati palori.
Cuss'iu, senza rimediu terrenu,
unu su dintra e n'autru paru fori;
su tuttu mestu e mustrumi serenu:
la vucca ridi e chiangimi lu cori.

O VERA E SULA BEDDA, IN CUI RELUCI

O vera e sula bedda, in cui reluci
quant'essiri bellizza mai potissi,
chi cussì puramenti netta e duci
corpu non fora mai chi la capissi,
in tia in la sua essenzia reluci
e, quandu in tuttu da l'autri spirissi,
tu, comu luci s'adduma di luci,
lu mundu di bellizza addumirissi.

A GRASS GROWN IN SARDINIA, NAY A POISON

A grass grown in Sardinia, nay a poison,
will make those tasting it die laughing.
There are no Galen antidotes for it,
nor magic words by Esculapius.
Likewise, without an earthly cure for it,
I'm one inside, outside another man:
I feel depressed, but look serene outside,
my mouth is laughing, but I weep inside.

O TRUE AND ONLY BEAUTY IN WHOM SHINES

O true and only beauty in whom shines
the highest form that beauty can achieve,
and that no other body can contain
in such a delicate and sweet proportion,
in you its essence is so paramount,
that if it faded fully from all others,
just as a flame starts from another flame,
your beauty would the universe inflame.

SUSPIRU, TU CHI NESCI DI DDU PETTU

Suspiru, tu chi nesci di ddu pettu
und'è lu cori miu chiusu e fermatu,
dimmi chi fa, siddu si sta in dilettu,
siddu chiù pensa a lu miu amaru statu!
E quandu torni a l'amatu ricettu,
com'hai a tornari d'airu accumpagnatu,
per fari un gestu ch'a intrambu sia accettu
in compagnia ti porta lu miu ciatu!

IU MORU, E STA MURTALI 'NFIRMITATI

Iu moru, e sta murtali 'nfirmitati
nun si canusci mancu pri l'effetti;
cussì cui pri veneni terminati
senz'autri signi a la morti si metti;
mortu chi sugnu, Amici, mi spaccati,
chi 'ntra lu cori, unni lu mali stetti,
la venefica mia pinta ci asciati,
lu tossicu chi fu, cui ci lu detti.

O SIGH, YOU WHO COME FROM INSIDE THAT CHEST

O sigh, you who come from inside that chest
where my poor heart is solidly enchained,
tell me what my love's doing, if she's glad,
if she still thinks of my state of despair!
And when you do return to your loved nest,
as you must be accompanied by air,
perform a deed that we would welcome both:
as a companion take along my breath.

I'M DYING AND THIS FATAL MALADY

I'm dying and this fatal malady
cannot be recognized by its effects,
just like when someone's killed by poisoning,
which does not give a clue as to the cause;
Once I am dead, my friends, split me apart,
for in my heart which housed my love disease
you'll find the face of my own poisoner,
the kind she used and who gave it to her.

DI PROPIA MANU ST'OPRA PINSI AMURI

Di propia manu st'opra pinsi Amuri
per farisi adurari iddu per diu:
macinau la bellizza, li coluri;
la grazia per pinzeddu ci serviu.
Poi chi cu milli travagghi e suduri
cussì divina immagini compliu,
ndi iu idolatra com'era pitturi
e ci sacrificau lu cori miu.

L'URA CH'IMPRESSU VIDIRI M'INGEGNU

L'ura ch'impressu vidiri m'ingegnu
la facci chi si guarda per disiu,
s'altera e turba e cu negghia di sdegnu
muta la bedda forma chi desiu;
ed iu in estasi vaiu e poi in mia vegnu:
s'è idda e s'iu sugn'iu criu e non criu.
Guarda chi gran contrarietati tegnu,
quandu la viu chiù mancu la viu.

WITH ITS OWN HANDS LOVE PAINTED THIS GOOD WORK

With its own hands Love painted this good work
in order to be worshippped as a god.
He ground out beauty and the colors too,
and utilized grace as a painting brush.
Then after toiling in a thousand ways,
he wrought an image that was so divine,
the painter changed to lover of his art,
and offered her a sacrifice: my heart.

THE MOMENT I MOVE CLOSER TO HER FACE

The moment I move closer to her face,
following my desire to see her better,
she grows perturbed and, veiled by clouds of scorn,
she alters that fair mien that I pine for.
So I taste bliss and then return in me.
That she is she and I am I, I vow
and disavow. What a confusing mess!
When I see more of her, I see her less.

S'iu di lu focu to sugn'arsu e persu,
comu nun senti lu to propriu arduri?
Anzi intornu lu cori, e d'ogni versu
d'eternu jelu ti circundi, e muri?
Sta qualitati, e st'effettu diversu
su propriamenti celesti favuri;
Cussì lu Suli scalfa l'universu,
ed iddu nun ha puntu di caluri.

LA MIA DISGRAZIA TUA DISGRAZIA FU

La mia disgrazia tua disgrazia fu,
pacenzia undi rimediu non ci pò,
chi, senza aviri ormai speranza chiù,
perdi ognunu di nui l'intentu so.
Sii costanti, ch'iu quali fui su,
nè di l'essiri miu mi movirò;
e, comu non poi tu n'essiri tu,
accussì non pozzu iu n'essiri to.

If I'm consumed and burned by your harsh fire

If I'm consumed and burned by your harsh fire,
how is it that you don't feel your own ardor?
Indeed, have you surrounded, nay walled in,
your very heart with everlasting ice?
This quality and this arcane effect
are truly favors by the gods bestowed;
the Sun the universe warms up this way,
and does not feel the heat of its own ray.

My hardship was a hardship for you too

My hardship was a hardship for you too,
—patience's a must where remedies fall short—
that both of us who have lost every hope,
have also lost the sight of our objective.
Be constant, for I am the man I was,
nor will I ever change the way I feel.
And as you cannot be other than you,
I can't belong to anyone but you.

SUPRA LI NOTI FERMI DI LU CORI

Supra li noti fermi di lu cori,
stabili e saudu in non mutarsi mai,
fannu li mei penseri varii cori,
contrapuntandu cui pocu e cui assai;
e tu, memoria, a li vuci canori
ci porti lu compassu e cu iddi vai
cantandu ducimenti sti palori:
sia beneditta l'ura chi l'amai!

CORI MIU, IN CELU PROPIA NON CI TROVI

Cori miu, in celu propia non ci trovi
signu chi di fermizza ndi conorta:
la luna muta formi in vecchi e novi,
lu suli ha la sua strata dritta e torta
e in ogni stidda varii aspetti provi
chi, girandu, lu celu leva e porta.
Chi sarrà di cui amamu? non si movi?
uh uh per nui, chi la speranza è morta.

40

Upon the Firm Notes of My Stable Heart

Upon the firm notes of my stable heart
that follows its unchanging, steady course,
my thoughts intone some varied choruses
and counterpoint some greatly and some less.
And you, my memory, as the maestro
conduct each voice and sing along with them,
and this refrain harmoniously repeat:
"The hour I fell in love now consecrate!"

Dear Heart, There Are No Inklings in the Sky

Dear heart, there are no inklings in the sky,
suggesting comforting stability.
The Moon will change its shape from old to new,
the Sun will run a straight and crooked path,
and in each star new aspects you will see,
which show or disappear as the sky turns.
What of the one we love? She's motionless!*
We are bereft of hope. Oh woe to us!

* If the woman he loves does not move, disobeying the movement that is the order
of the universe, she will not be able to change toward him.

Cu duci modi mi lighi e ncatini

Cu duci modi mi lighi e ncatini,
tal chi li sensi mei non su chiù soi:
fa' di mia scheltu, ingrata chi mai fini,
o in atomi risolvimi, si poi!
E si non basti, st'ossa, carni e vini
risolvili a lu minimu chi voi,
chi ddu minimu stissu senza fini
amirà estremu li bellizzi toi.

Mi formu di tia un'ecu in ogni locu

Mi formu di tia un'ecu in ogni locu
e parimi ch'iu parlu e tu respundi.
S'iu cantu o chiangiu pr'esalari un pocu,
sentu li canti e chianti toi profundi;
s'in sugghiuzzi, suspiri o vuci sfocu,
tu in sugghiuzzi, suspiri e vuci abbundi.
o fintu beni, o travagghiatu iocu,
m'immaginu fruirti e non viu undi.

WITH HER SWEET WAYS SHE BINDS AND KEEPS ME CHAINED

With your sweet ways you bind and keep me chained
so that my senses are no longer mine.
Reduce me to a skeleton, ingrate,
who never stop, or turn me into atoms,
and if that's not enough, this flesh, these bones,
these veins, reduce to the bare minimum,
for even with the smallest part of me
your beauty I will love eternally.

YOUR ECHO I'VE CREATED IN MY HEAD

Your echo I've created in my head
and as I speak I think I hear you answer.
If I should sing or cry to find relief,
I hear your songs and cries inside of me;
if I sob, sigh or cry to vent my woes,
you will respond with sobs and sighs and cries.
O fictive goodness, o tormenting play,
I think I have you, but where I can't say.

O, SI PER SORTI AVISSI FATTU DIU

O, si per sorti avissi fattu Diu
reciprocu l'amuri fra di nui,
nè cori vostru ci fussi nè miu,
ma fussimu vui ed iu unu e nun dui.
Cert'è, ch'ancor chi locu ndi spartiu,
la vogghia e lu disiu nd'uniria chiui:
ora iu senza di vui sugnu senz'iu
e vui senza di mia siti iu e vui.

SI LI CELESTI SFERI SU GIRATI

Si li celesti sferi su girati
di li chiù beddi spiriti e chiù puri,
sferi di lu miu celu, ch'avanzati
chist'autri celi in forza ed in splenduri,
cui vi duna lu motu? undi spirati
a un giru d'occhi lu divinu arduri?
Ah, chi ben sentu, non mi lu negati,
chi per vui diventau spiritu Amuri!

O IF BY DESTINY GOD MADE THE LOVE

O if by destiny God made the love
between the two of us reciprocal,
there would not be a heart that's yours or mine,
but you and I would be one heart, not two.
For sure, though distance's keeping us apart,
our will and our desires unite us more:
Now I'm without myself, not having you,
and you, without me, are both me and you.

IF THE CELESTIAL SPHERES ARE MADE TO TURN

If the celestial spheres are made to turn
by the most beautiful and purest spirits,
o spheres of my own heaven who surpass
those other spheres in beauty and in splendor,
who gives you strength to move? Where do you turn
your heavenly fire as you move your eyes?
Ah, I feel it now, do not deny me some!
Because of you, Love spirit has become.

Chista Medusa ch'in petra mi muta

Chista Medusa ch'in petra mi muta
pri fari a la durizza sua maramma,
di mia farindi cauci è risuluta,
chi per focu si coci e pr'acqua inxiamma;
E tali morti a dunarmi s'aiuta
chi, mentri mi consuma a dramma a dramma,
né pr'acqua, né pri focu mai s'astuta,
anzi pr'intrambu dubbla la mia xiamma.

Planeta und'hannu iornu l'occhi mei

Planeta und'hannu iornu l'occhi mei,
cui di l'aspettu to mi fici fori?
o felici tri voti amanti e sei,
ch'avendu a impeiurari primu mori!
Benchì per sorti e vogghia di li dei
tu sì in Sicilia ed iu in terra di Mori,
t'aduru cu li spirti afflitti e rei:
li zo chi non pò lu corpu fa lu cori.

This my Medusa that's transforming me*

This my Medusa that's transforming me
to stone to show the might of her own hardness
has made a vow to turn me into lime,
which cooks with fire and with water burns.
and she is striving to cause me such death
that while consuming me bit by small bit
her flame can't be put out by water or fire,
but both contrive to make my own burn higher

Planet who bring light to my weary eyes

Planet who bring light to my weary eyes,
who drove me far away and out of sight?
Three, nay, six times as happy is the lover,
who knowing things will worsen, will die first.
Although by gods' desires or destiny
I'm in Moors' lands,** and you on Sicily,
with my afflicted soul, I pray to you:
what bodies cannot do, the heart will do.

---

* Medusa was a most beautiful woman who was turned by Athena into a monster
with snakes as hair. She had the power to turn to stone anyone who chanced to look at
her.

** Moors' land refers to the poet's two-year imprisonment in Algiers after he was
captured by pirates. He was there from 1578 to 1580 and shared a cell with Miguel
Cervantes, the author of the *Don Quijote de la Mancha*. It is believed he wrote many of
the poems in *Celia* during his captivity.

RIVENI, SI RECRIA E SI RESTAURA

Riveni, si recria e si restaura
undi tu appari intornu lu paisi,
l'airu di lu to gratu oduri ciaura,
ciurisci lu terrenu chi scalpisi.
Di lu to lustru lu suli s' innaura
e lucindi la luna d'ogni misi:
sulu a la mia fortuna per duci aura
mai veni, o per sant'Ermu a lu caucisi.

S'IU MUTAI MODU, STILU, ABITU E FORMA,

S'iu mutai modu, stilu, abitu e forma,
dati la culpa a la nimica mia,
chi mi s'ha fattu so e, vigghia o dorma,
comu un camaleonti mi varia.
Idda è regula mia, idda è mia norma
e cu la vista affettuusa o ria
mi muta e smuta, mi forma e trasforma,
e quantu voli vali e fa di mia.

48

WHEN YOU APPEAR AROUND THE COUNTRYSIDE

When you appear around the countryside
the world's restored, reborn, rejuvenated;
the air exhales your welcome, sweet perfume,
the earth on which you tread begins to bloom.
Your splendor gives the sun its golden rays
and every month the moon partakes of it.
Only to my storm you never alight
as a sweet breeze or as St. Elmo's light.*

IF I HAVE CHANGED MY WAYS, STYLE, HABIT, FORM

If I have changed my ways, style, habit, form,
give the blame rightly to my enemy
who made me hers and who, awake or sleeping,
has made a true chameleon out of me.
She is my rule, my norm she represents,
and with her harsh or loving looks I'm made
and then unmade, formed and transformed, at will.
She makes of me whatever suits her will.

* St. Elmo's light is a sudden light that appears on top of the mast after a storm signalling the end.

MI RUDU, MI MINUZZU, ANZI MI STENDU

Mi rudu, mi minuzzu, anzi mi stendu,
com'oru per trafilu assuttigghiandu
e non m'avvinciu mai, né mai mi rendu,
sempri chiu disiusi l'ali spandu.
Timu chiù, comu diventau chiangendu
Egeria ciumi e vuci Ecu gridandu,
iu, mentri pensu e pensari pretendu,
non mi risolva in penseri pensandu.

FUI PRISU IN RISGUARDARI LA GRANDIZZA

Fui prisu in risguardari la grandizza
di vostra divinissima figura:
"l'eburnea frunti, la deorata trizza,
la vucca cinta d'impernati mura;
l'occhi, und'amuri cu li Grazii sgrizza ;
e spira grazii e amuri a cui v' adura.
Vui siti, donna, specchiu di bellizza,
miraculu di Diu, d'arti e natura.

I STRUGGLE, BREAK APART, NAY, SPREAD MYSELF

I struggle, break apart, nay, spread myself
like ever thinning, melting, golden wire
and I do not give up, nor yet surrender,
spreading my wings to follow my desire.
I fear that as Egeria stream became *
out of her tears, and Echo voice from screaming,**
while I am thinking and in thought persist,
I'll fade and only as a thought exist.

I WAS IMPRISONED AS I GAZED UPON

I was imprisoned as I gazed upon
the greatness of your figure most divine:
the ivory-hued forehead, the golden tress,
the mouth surrounded by pearl-colored walls,
the eyes wherein Love with the Graces plays,
inspiring love and grace to those who love you.
Lady, true beauty you reflect indeed:
of art and nature, you're a godly deed.

*Egeria was a nymph who transformed herself into a stream weeping for the death of King Numa.
** Echo was transformed into a voice as she called out her love for Narcissus.

TEGNU CENT'OCCHI A CHIDDI D'ARGO EGUALI

Tegnu cent'occhi a chiddi d'Argo eguali,
ch'a la mia donna sintinedda fannu,
contra di cui letargu nun ci vali,
né si ponnu addummisciri cu 'ngannu;
O chiusi, o aperti hannu vicenna tali,
ch'a la sua posta a lu so tempu stannu,
li chiusi pri nun vidiri lu mali,
e l'aperti pri chiangiri lu dannu.

PETRI CHI FABRICATI L'AUTI MURA

Petri chi fabricati l'auti mura
undi lu beni miu chiusa teniti,
comu, secundu la vostra natura,
a la gran focu miu non vi cociti?
Comu a li mei suspiri c'è dimura?
comu a lu chiantu miu lippu faciti?
a chi occultarmi l'amata figura
vui, chi nè gustu nè sensu nd'haviti?

I HAVE A HUNDRED EYES THE SAME AS ARGUS

I have a hundred eyes the same as Argus,*
which keep my woman under constant watch.
They're not affected by fatigue at all,
nor can they fall asleep through some deceit;
But closed or open they have such travails
that they remain forever poised, on guard:
the closed eyes not to see the evil done,
the open ones to weep for what went on.

O STONES THAT MAKE HIGH WALLS INSIDE OF WHICH

O stones that make high walls inside of which
you keep my own beloved bliss well hidden,
how is it that according to your nature
you do not burn before my searing flame?
How can you hesitate before my sighs?
How can you let moss grow before my cries?
You, who can't feel or profit from her grace,
why do you hide from me that lovely face?

MI SONNAI CHI VUI ED IU, PATRUNA MIA, MORTI

Mi sonnai chi vui ed iu, patruna mia, morti,
a l'infernu iamu condannati:
iu, perchì cosa celesti vulia,
vui per la vostra troppu crudeltati.
Vui tantu eravu sazia di mia,
chi festa vi paria quantu si pati;
iu, per la vostra vista e compagnia,
stari non mi cridia fra li dannati.

VENIMI IN SONNU, POI CHI NON VOI IN VIGGHIU

Venimi in sonnu, poi chi non voi in vigghiu,
puru chi viia a tia, gabbami e fingi,
chi si ben l'umbra indarnu abbrazzu e pigghiu,
l'amanti un duci ingannu lu suspingi.
E si burlatu, ohimè, poi mi risbigghiu
e a lu spariri to l'alma si tingi,
purro' laudarmi chiù d'un to assimigghiu
chi di tia stissa, ch'a morti mi spingi.

I DREAMED THAT YOU AND I WERE DEAD

I dreamed that you and I were dead, my Lady,
and that we had descended into hell:
for wanting a celestial creature, I,
but you, for your excessive cruelty.
You were so fed up with my company
that all the suffering down there was fun;
but with you there, I did not mind at all.
I did not think I was damned down in hell.

AS YOU WON'T COME TO ME AWAKE, COME IN

As you won't come to me awake, come in
my dreams. Deceive me, but let me see you,
for even if a shadow I embrace,
a lover is spurred on by such deceits.
And if when I awaken I am fooled,
and my soul saddens as you disappear,
I can rejoice in your reflection more
than in yourself who drive me to death's door.

* Argus was mythological being who had a hundred eyes and never slept, keeping always a few of his eyes open.

MI GIRA NTORNU LA MENTI UN PENSERI

Mi gira ntornu la menti un penseri
chi comu senia mai cessa un istanti,
ma cu carlisi di doluri veri
ligati a cordi di speranzi erranti,
scindi ed acchiana e torna e scindi arreri
a lu cori, undi surginu li chianti,
e l'inchi e porta chini di chimeri,
e poi li cala di frutti vacanti.

LIGAMI, BENI MIU, LIGAMI E STRINCI

Ligami, beni miu, ligami e strinci
cu milli, si non basta un sulu lazzu:
si liga cui la Curti lu costrinci,
si liga cui si serra gamba o brazzu.
Si liga in guerra cui si pigghia e vinci,
liga cui è folli e la medulla ha a sguazzu:
ed iu, per lu to amuri chi m'avvinci,
su reu, su infirmu, su scavu e su pazzu.

INSIDE MY HEAD A THOUGHT IS CHURNING ROUND

Inside my head a thought is churning round
like the *noria* turning without pause,
which with small buckets laden with true woes,
tied up with ropes of fleeting expectations,
climbs and descends and then comes up again
to the poor heart where weeping then begins
and fills the buckets up with empty dreams
and then bereft of fruits it lowers them.

CHAIN ME, MY LOVE, O CHAIN ME AND HOLD TIGHT

Chain me, my love, o chain me and hold tight.
A thousand ropes use, if one's not enough.
People chain those whom Justice has found guilty,
they chain the man whose leg or arm is sawn,
they chain the soldier who has lost in war,
they chain the madman whose poor brain is loose,
and I, for the effects your love has had,
I'm guilty, sick, a slave I am, and mad.

Lavati la testuzza, vita mia,
chiù bedda chi non vitti a Febu santu;
ma mi fai ingiuria, ch'essiri vorria
cosa chi ti servissi tantu o quantu.
Sapuni, a li to manu squagghiria;
vacili, appariria la grazia intantu;
o, a nenti a nenti, mi farria liscìa,
cinniri st'arsu cori, acqua lu chiantu.

O WASH YOUR LOVELY HEAD, MY LOVE, FOR I

O wash your lovely head, my love, for I
never did see the like of yours on Phoebus;
but you displease me for I would have liked
to be of service to you in some way.
As soap I'd liquefy inside your hands,
as basin I'd reflect your graces fair,
or at the very least I could be lye*:
ash from my burned heart, water as I cry.

---

*Note. Lye is a cleaning mixture that was used until recently in Sicily for washing clothes. It combines ashes and water.

Libru secundu di canzuni amurusi siciliani

Second Book of Sicilian Love Songs

Gira lu cori comu lignu a tornu
supra dui perni, speranza e disiu;
undi fermu la vista e movu intornu
non scopru umbra di paci, nè disviu.
Per tia, ciatu, di morti in vita tornu
e cu tia l'afflitt'anima recriu,
nè mi pari ch'è iornu chiddu iornu
chi lu to suli luciri non viu.

CU SUTTILI VENENU AMURI APPESTA

Cu suttili venenu amuri appesta
ed undi tocca eternamenti dura,
cussì un cani arraggiatu cui molesta
ci attacca un mali chi mai chiù si cura.
o vui, a cui Diu li iorna leti presta,
fuiti undi c'è amanti in fossa scura,
perchì, s'amuri poi di morti festa,
v'infettirà la stissa sepultura.

MY HEART REVOLVES LIKE WOOD AROUND THE LATHE

My heart revolves like wood around the lathe
held by two pins: my hope and my desire;
No matter where I turn my eyes, I see
no glimpse of peace or of distraction.
For you, my breath, I come from death to life
and this afflicted soul rejuvenate,
nor does it seems the day has dawned that day
when of your sun I don't see the bright ray.

WITH SUBTLE POISON LOVE INFECTS A MAN

With subtle poison Love infects a man
and where it touches it will last forever;
just like a rabid dog infects the one
molesting it with a disease that's fatal.
O you, whom God affords some happy days,
flee from the somber grave where lovers are,
for if love should survive beyond their death,
love will infect the grave with its last breath.

AMURI UN GHIORNU SI DELIBERAU

Amuri un ghiornu si deliberau
di vidiri lu intrinsecu di mia
e tuttu in pezzi mi ruppi e tagghiau,
medicu accortu, accorta notomia!
D'un sulu effettu si maravigghiau
quantu l'invitta sua potenzia sia,
chi, vivu, senza cori mi truvau
fattu sequaci di la donna mia.

LA NOTTI IN SONNU, DORMENDU, T' ABBRAZZU

La notti in sonnu, dormendu, t' abbrazzu;
criu abbrazzari a tia e abbrazzu lu ventu:
o chi gran chiantu e gran lamentu fazzu,
o chi gran pena a lu miu cori sentu!
Poi mi risbigghiu, la nfingiu e la sfrazzu,
forsi vigghiandu passassi lu stentu;
- ma non mi servi, su impintu a lu lazzu:
dorma o non dorma, vigghia lu tormentu.

One day Love pondered and decided that

One day Love pondered and decided that
he wanted to see my internal parts
and so he broke and cut me into pieces:
a careful surgeon, good anatomist!
He was amazed about one thing, however:
how mighty and unvanquished was his power,
for though I was alive, he found no heart:
it had gone to my Lady from the start.

At night asleep I hug you in my dreams.

At night asleep I hold you in my dreams.
I think I'm hugging you, but I hug air.
O what sad weeping, what grief-stricken cry,
o what great sorrow enters then my heart!
Then I awaken, feign and make believe
it's nothing, hoping the distress would end.
But it's no use: I am bound to the chains:
awake or sleeping, my torment remains.

A LU SULI IN LIUNI CHIÙ COCENTI

A lu suli in liuni chiù cocenti
paru una importunissima cicala,
chi non ha bucca e campa sulamenti
di la ruggiata chi di celu cala;
e forma aprendu lu pettu l'accenti
ch'ispira l' airu battutu cu l'ala,
accenti nati d'arduri chi senti
fina chi l'alma cu lu cantu esala.

AD OGNI SGUARDU TO FORMI UNA STILLA

Ad ogni sguardu to formi una stilla
e ad ogni risu crii milli aurori,
ad un passu Eolu lu mari tranquilla,
a un motu scopri infiniti tesori.
ietta ligustri e rosi ogni mascilla,
la vucca d'ambra odorati calori.
o forgia undi si fundi amuri e stilla,
o isca, amu e cimedda di li cori!

DURING THE HOTTEST DOG DAYS OF THE YEAR

During the hottest dog days of the year,
I seem to be a bothersome cicada
who has no mouth and lives upon the dew
that from the sky descends upon the earth,
and forms by opening its chest those sounds,
that the air beaten with its wings provokes,
sounds that are born from burning that he feels,
until his soul in singing he exhales.

WITH EVERY LITTLE GLANCE YOU FORM A STAR

With every little glance you form a star;
with every smile you form a thousand dawns;
with every step you soothe the raging sea;
with every move you show us endless treasures.
From your cheeks blossom roses and sweet tendrils,
and from your mouth breath scented with sweet
                              amber.
O furnace where love you distill and fuse,
o fishing pole of hearts, o bait and noose.

UN TEMPU LA FORTUNA MI DISFICI

Un tempu la fortuna mi disfici,
dipoi m'apparsi e dissi: "comu stai?"
Iu, chi mi vitti luntanu d'amici,
comu la vitti, tuttu m' alligrai;
dissi: "Fortuna, perchì non mi dici
si di l'intuttu abbandunatu m'hai?".
Ntendi ccà la risposta chi mi fici:
"Cui teni fidi a Diu non peri mai".

QUALI CAMALEONTI, CHI D'OGN'URA

Quali camaleonti, chi d'ogn'ura
varii culuri mustra in una fogghia,
tali mia donna in unica figura
dimustra variu vultu e varia vogghia.
Ma chiddu sulu d'airu si procura
li propii civi, e chista di mia dogghia;
e mi tratteni cu tali mistura
la morti, chi di vita non mi spogghia.

SOME TIME AGO MY FORTUNE HAD DESTROYED ME

Some time ago my Fortune had destroyed me.
Afterward she appeared and said: "How are you?"
There were no friendly faces when I saw her.
So, full of cheer I turned to her and said :
"Fortune, why don't you let me know for sure
if you have totally abandoned me."
Listen to what she said as her reply:
"Who ever trusts in God will never die."

LIKE A CHAMELEON WHO SITTING ON A LEAF

Like a chameleon who sitting on a leaf
displays at every hour different colors,
such is my lady who displays changed looks,
and varied wants while being only one.
But while the animal finds food in air,
she only feeds herself upon my woes;
and death detains me with so strange a blend
that my life it will neither take nor end.

IN CHISTA SCENA DI LA NOSTRA MENTI

In chista scena di la nostra menti
Amuri vesti e fa li persunaggi
d'omini donni, di iudei valenti,
d'arditi vecchi e di patruni paggi.
Ognunu fingi e voluntariu menti
l'abiti differenti a li curaggi,
e li chiui umiliati e impazienti
di bravi rappresentanu e di saggi.

NUN È LU SONNU IMMAGINI DI MORTI

Nun è lu sonnu immagini di morti,
è vita di l'amanti, a quantu viu:
mi mi fa lu vigilari milli torti,
chi o ceiu, o fuiu, o canzu, o accecu, o sviu.
Cu l'occhi chiusi ottegnu per mia sorti
duci confortu o segretu disviu:
sentu, audu, abbrazzu, vasu, stringiu forti.
E quali cuntintizza chiù disiu?

UPON THE STAGE OF OUR IMAGINATION

Upon the stage of our imagination
Love dresses every character, and changes
men into women, Jews to faithful men.
Thus lords become mere serfs, old folks grow bold,
and every one pretends and willingly
embraces habits that are different.
So the most humbled and impatient then
perform the part of wise and honest men.

OUR SLEEP IS NOT AN IMAGE OF COLD DEATH

Our sleep is not an image of cold death;
it's life for lovers, as I can discern.
Being awake is source of many woes
that make me flee, hide, lose my sight or way.
But with eyes closed I'm able to obtain
sweet consolation and concealed relief:
I feel and hear, I hug, embrace and kiss.
Can I wish for a greater joy than this?

Ivi a l' infernu per vidiri forsi

Ivi a l' infernu per vidiri forsi
lu miu gran focu putiri acqua farsi,
e quantu potti suttilmenti scorsi
di puntu in puntu e truvai vampi scarsi.
Videndu lu miu focu, già si morsi
lu focu eternu ed ogni vampa s' arsi,
tali chi senza dubbiu m' accorsi
chi simili a lu miu mai focu parsi.

Mentri lu tempu misurava l'uri

Mentri lu tempu misurava l'uri
e di l'amanti cuntava li stenti,
dissi parlandu sutt'umbri e figuri:
"virtù è spiranza e la rina tormenti."
Ntisi e ci ruppi la mpulletta Amuri
e suggiunsi adiratu incontinenti:
"mmatula cunti e mmatula misuri,
ch'un veru amuri dura eternamenti".

I WENT TO HELL TO SEE IF I, SOMEHOW

I went to hell to see if I, somehow,
could change my fire into water there,
and with great care, I thoroughly searched through
the place and found that flames were scarce indeed.
Seeing the fire that I held inside, all flames
of the eternal fire faded out.
So that without a doubt I can opine
that there has never been a flame like mine.

WHILE TIME WAS BUSY MEASURING THE HOURS

While time was busy measuring the hours
and counting lovers' harsh frustrations,
he uttered, speaking through veiled metaphors:
"The glass is hope, but torment is the sand."
Love heard the words and broke the hourglass,
adding immediately and angrily:
"Counting and measuring is vanity,
for a true love lasts for eternity."

LA CANDILA MAI S'AUDI NÈ SI SENTI

La candila mai s'audi nè si senti,
sula s'ardi e consuma a pocu a pocu;
ma poi a la fini su li soi tormenti
e pari chi cantassi e stassi in iocu.
Cussì sugn'iu, ch'infini, arsu e cucenti
da li vostr' occhi a cui chiangendu invocu,
pari chi canta, ma intrinsicamenti
su vuci estremi di cui mori in focu.

CERTI ZIFFATI DI CIAURUSU VENTU

Certi ziffati di ciaurusu ventu
mi vennu ntra la facci ad ura ad ura,
chi mi dunanu vita e nutrimentu
comu fa a lu scursuni per natura.
Cui osservassi a ddu puntu e a ddu momentu
ch'amuri tanta grazia mi procura,
truviria, beni miu, cussì, e nun mentu,
chi tu suspiri o chi tu ciati allura.

THE CANDLE NEVER HEARS ITSELF, NOR FEELS

The candle never hears itself, nor feels.
It simply burns, and slowly dies away.
Its torments come, however, at the end,
when it appears to sing and to feel glad.
That's how I am, that at the end, consumed,
set blazing by your eyes to whom I pray.
I seem to sing, but truly, I proclaim,
mine's the last sound of one who dies aflame.

FROM TIME TO TIME I FEEL UPON MY FACE

From time to time I feel upon my face
some intermittent breaths of sweet, cool wind
which seem to give me nourishment and life,
as happens with the snakes. in nature's realm.
If someone were observing time and place,
how love was giving me such wondrous grace,
they would find out, my love, and I'm not lying,
they were your breathing or perhaps your sighing.

ANCORA N'ERA NATU E PATIA DANNI

Ancora n'era natu e patia danni:
la causa lu dimustra, cridimindi,
perchì fortuna cu soi fausi inganni
milli fiati lu iornu mi vindi.
Sunnu in tanta miseria li mei anni,
chi l'unu mali acchiana e l'autru scindi;
poi chi non hannu fini li mei affanni,
corpu, di riposari spisatindi.

SU TORNATU LANTERNA, UNDI SI SERRA

Su tornatu lanterna, undi si serra
una lucerna ch'ardi in ogni locu:
l'ha fattu Amuri per darimi guerra
e tormentarmi a l'amurusu iocu.
Lu mecciu ch'ardi e ch'a lu focu afferra
e lu miu cori estintu a pocu a pocu,
l'afflittu pettu è lu vasu di terra,
ogghiu lu sangu e vui siti lu focu.

I WAS NOT EVEN BORN AND I HAD WOES

I was not even born and I had woes;
the cause, believe me, demonstrates as much,
for fortune with its thousand, false deceits,
sells me a thousand times a day. My years
have fallen into such harsh misery
a pain increases as another fades;
since there's no end in sight to all my woes,
body, it's useless hoping for repose.

I HAVE BECOME A LANTERN INSIDE WHICH

I have become a lantern inside which
there is a light that's burning through and through:
it was love who declared this war on me,
to make me suffer in the loving game.
The burning wick that to the flame's attached
is my poor heart who's dying bit by bit.
My wretched chest's the lantern made of clay;
my blood's the oil and you're the flame, I say.

IU AMU, AMARU MIA, IU AMU, IU AMU

Iu amu, amaru mia, iu amu, iu amu,
nè in miu rimediu aiutu vali o vasi.
Per disamari, comu non disamu,
l'occasioni lu tuppu si rasi.
Miseru invanu mi lamentu e sclamu
si vulau l'apa lu ferru rimasi:
iu su pisci incappatu a lu vostr'amu,
quantu chiui mi ritiru chiù mi trasi.

STAVI A LU TAVULERI COMU UN ROCCU

Stavi a lu tavuleri comu un roccu
e poi ristasti in percia comu un duccu;
prontu per difensari cu lu stoccu
et autru vinni e riminau lu giuccu.
Chi ti iuvau li manu haviri a croccu
e caminari supra lu trabuccu,
si quandu stavi apuntu a fari troccu
ci vinni nautru e fici truccu mbuccu?

78

I LOVE, OH WRETCHED ME, I LOVE, I LOVE

I love, oh wretched me, I love, I love,
there was no cure for me, nor will there be.
The time for the unloving's come and gone
and I cannot unlove you, that is clear.
I moan and cry in wretchedness in vain,
for if the bee has flown, the sting remains.
I am a fish entangled in your net:
the more I run the more entwined I get.

YOU STOOD THERE ON THE PLAIN LIKE A HARD ROCK

You stood there on the plain like a hard rock
and then you were left dangling like a jerk.
You were all ready to protect your stock,
but someone else arrived your claim to work.
What good was to pretend you were a Jock,
stalking your prey and ever on the lurk,
if when you were about the bird to pluck
another man came in and stole your duck?

BEN VILI E BEN MANCATU AFFATTU FORA

Ben vili e ben mancatu affattu fora
si chiù sciaurassi a tia nè fatti toi,
sollenni mancatura di parola:
non sì voluta e dici chi non voi!
Oh si avanti vidia quantu viju hora,
caca-e-passa facia comu lu groi,
pinnula liscia nnaurata di fora,
dintra impastata di feli e d'aloi!

MI IUVAU, MI IUVAU L'ESSIRI LICCU

Mi iuvau, mi iuvau l'essiri liccu,
la bedda a un miu petittu consentiu;
ci vasai la vuccuzza e restu siccu
comu a lu vasu l'alma non mi xiu.
Hora chi campu su beatu e riccu:
per memoria et eternu gustu miu
mi vasu iu propriu, scrusciu e mi perliccu
li labbra undi lu beni mi trasiu.

I WOULD BE A GREAT COWARD WITHOUT FAITH

I would be a great coward without faith
if ever I came near to smell your scent,
impostor, who can't keep your promises:
you claim you do not want, but you're unwanted.
Oh if I saw before what I see now,
I would have shit and run as the crane does.
You are a smooth and golden pill, outside,
with aloe mixed and poison on the inside.

IT PAID! TO BE INSISTENT REALLY PAID

It paid! To be insistent really paid,
for my fair beauty granted my desire;
I kissed her little mouth and I am stunned
that my poor soul did not abandon me.
As I survived, I live in bliss and wealth:
through memory for my eternal pleasure
I kiss myself, I smack my lips and savor
the spot on which my goodness left her flavor.

Cussì bedda tarantula et esperta

Cussì bedda tarantula et esperta
per muzzicari a mia si fici Amuri,
chi la vina truvau chiù propia e certa
d'inquietarmi la menti e l'homuri.
E per chiù doghia, cui la nota incerta
ch'in parti abbalchiria li miei doluri,
è mia nimica e, attali chi non verta,
quand'iu cantu vorria, sona tenuri.

Talmenti Amuri mi travaghia e sversa

Talmenti Amuri mi travaghia e sversa,
ch'amanti mai non happi peiu statu,
perchì su comu cui dormi a la mbersa,
chi lu mazzamareddu l'ha occupatu.
Quietu di quieti assai riversa,
d'un sonnu di mal'umbri tempestatu,
e viju e ntendu, ma la forza è persa;
vorria gridari aiutu, e n'haiu ciatu.

LOVE TURNED HIMSELF INTO A BEAUTIFUL

Love turned himself into a beautiful,
expert tarantula to come bite me,
and found the vein most suitable and sure
to trouble both my mind and disposition.
And to my greater woe, the one who could,
in part, relieve my troubles is my foe.
To cause me much distress he clearly vowed:
when I want music low, his voice grows loud.

LOVE HAS REDUCED ME TO SO POOR A STATE

Love has reduced me to so poor a state:
no lover ever was in sadder straits.
I'm like a man who sleeps when he should wake
because the incubus has taken him.
Forlorn, prey to the tortured quietude
of dreams infested with ill-omened ghosts,
I am bereft of strength, but feel and see.
I want to scream, but I've no breath in me.

QUANDU PENSU A L'ANTICA MIA FUDDIA

Quandu pensu a l'antica mia fuddia,
ed a lu tempu malamenti spisu,
restu privu di sensi, anzi vurria,
chi vivu vivu in sciammi fussi misu.
Ma quandu pensu chi sulu per mia
Cristu fu cu tri chiova in Cruci appisu,
st'ingratu cori a pezzi scippiria
ch'a un Diu, chi tantu l'ama, ha tant'offisu.
Canzuni Sacra

CORI CHIANCI, PIRCHÌ? *PIRCHÌ SU AMANTI*

Cori chianci, pirchì? *Pirchì su amanti.*
Di cui? *D'una spietata, e sconoscenti.*
T'ama? *Nun m'ama, e di suspiri, e chianti*
mi pasci ogn'ura l'affannata menti.
L'amasti? *Ju l'amai firmu e custanti.*
Fusti pagatu? *Sì, di peni e stenti.*
Dimmi, in premiu chi avisti? *Amari chianti.*
E l'ami? *L'amu.* E chi nni speri? *Nenti.*

WHEN I REFLECT UPON MY ANCIENT FOLLY

When I reflect upon my ancient folly,
and on the time I wasted wretchedly,
I am completely stunned, indeed, I'd like
to be thrown into the live flames alive.
But when I think that only for my sake
Christ with three nails was hung upon the Cross,
I'd tear my heart in pieces from my chest
for so offending God who loves it best.
Sacred Song

WHY ARE YOU CRYING, HEART? *'CAUSE I'M IN LOVE*

Why are you crying, heart? *'cause I'm in love.*
With whom? *An ingrate with no heart at all.*
Does she love you? *She does not love me, no,*
and feeds my troubled mind with sighs and woe.
Did you love her? *With firm and constant heart.*
Were you repaid? *Yes, with great woes and strains.*
Tell me, what was your prize? *My bitter tears.*
Still love her? *Yes.* What hopes have you? *None, none.*

Sutta un niuru cipressu unni la luna
mannava appena i soi friddi rai,
cuntava li me peni ad una ad una,
na vuci sentu, e i me occhi alzai.
Uh! Uh! facia ntra chidd'aria bruna
dulurusu giacobbu amari lai!
Mi si ancora cuntraria furtuna!
Stu trivulu mancava a li me guai.

AMICI, AMICI, QUADARI, QUADARI

Amici, amici, quadari, quadari
Facitimi quadari di liscia,
Ca tutti quanti mi vogghiu squadari
Li robbi di la Vicaria.
Curriti, curriti, mastri pittinari
Purtati tutti pettini pri mia;
E s"un c'è corna, faciti sirrari
Li corna a chiddi chi 'nfussaru a mia.

BENEATH A SOMBER CYPRESS TREE WHEREIN

Beneath a somber cypress tree wherein
the Moon reflected barely its cold rays,
I counted all my troubles one by one.
I heard a voice and quickly raised my eyes.
Ooh, ooh! the owl's sorrowful lament
resounded woefully in the dark air.
My luck is still against me, still adverse!
That's all I needed to make matters worse!

MY FRIENDS, MY FRIENDS, CAULDRONS AND CAULDRONS

My friends, my friends, cauldrons and cauldrons
                                    bring,
many a cauldron full of lye prepare
for me because I want to wash away
the filthy clothes soiled in the Vicaria*;
Come running all of you, master comb makers,
bring all the combs you have in stock for me,
and if you cannot find horns** readily,
go saw the horns off those who buried me.

*The Vicaria was the notorious prison of Palermo.
** Horn is the material from which combs were made. Veneziano was playing with
the double meaning of "corna" venting his anger for being in prison against the "cornuti"
(cuckolds) who betrayed him. (See the intorduction).

Canzuni di sdegno

Songs of Contempt

Fra la mia lingua e la manu fu liga
di scriviri, né diri cosa vili;
né mai sappi appartarmi di la riga
d'amurusi, cortisi atti gentili.
Ora, ohimè, chi chiangiu la fatiga,
semu, la musa ed iu, fatti crudili:
chi Laura 'nfami, ch'insolenti striga
mi storciu, mi guastau, mi cangiau stili!

NON TI GLORIJRAI DI LU MIU MALI

Non ti glorijrai di lu miu mali,
Scortisi, disleali ed inhumana,
Chi da pietati, chi cu tia non vali,
Axhirò scala, pr'undi 'n celu acchiana.
Benchì firutu di colpi mortali,
Pari ch'ogni arti mi rinexxa vana;
Truvirò, truvirò dittami tali,
Chi mi xippa lu ferru e chi mi sana.

My Tongue and Hand Agreed Not to Write Down

My tongue and hand agreed not to write down
or ever say unworthy and vile things;
and I was always able not to stray
from loving rhymes and gentle civil deeds.
Alas, now that I'm crying for the effort
we have become unkind, my Muse and I,
for wicked Laura, a witch rude and vile,
twisted and ruined me, and changed my style.

You Will Not Gain Much Glory from My Woes

You will not gain much glory from my woes,
uncouth, disloyal and inhuman lady,
for mercy, which does not hold sway on you,
will find a stairway leading up to heaven.
Though I've been wounded with harsh, fatal blows,
and it appears all my attempts are vain,
still I will find, I'll find a way to pull
the sword out of my chest and my wound heal.

POI CHI ODDIARMI TI FU DATU IN SORTI

Poi chi oddiarmi ti fu datu in sorti,
ed a mia middi complimenti farti
ringrazia Amuri ad auti vuci forti;
e di tia lu miu cori si disparti!
Anzi, per tanti sdegni e tanti torti,
non sulamenti su' per oddiarti,
mentri chi campirò; poi di la morti
lu spirtu trovirai prontu a noiarti.

S'AUTRU DI TIA ND'OTTINNI E NDI RICIPPI

S'autru di tia nd'ottinni e ndi ricippi
Lu meghiu chi ti vitti e chi ti sappi,
Mula, ch'ad ogni fangu iochi e trippi,
Turdu, ch'ad ogni lazzu e riti 'ncappi
Fonti, chi cui non vosi non ci vippi,
Viti, chi d'ogni tempu hai middi rappi:
Lu primu fui chi t'happi, comu dippi!
Bedda guarnuta, ed hora cui nd'happ' happi.

Since it's your fate to have disdain for me

Since it's your fate to have disdain for me
and mine's to pay you many compliments,
you can thank Love with loud and grateful voice
for now my heart will take its leave from you.
Indeed, for all the many wrongs and scorn
not only am I ready to despise you
while I'm alive; but after I am dead,
you'll find my soul prepared to cause you dread.

If I obtained and got a thing from you

If I obtained and got a thing from you,
I got the better part I saw and knew:
Mule, who'll jump 'n play in mud without ado;
Thrush, who will stick to nets and noose like glue;
Fount, where all wanting drink will form a queue;
Grapevine, that grapes produce all seasons through;
I was the first who screwed you, Buckaroo,
and now, my cuckold, I am rid of you.

PER UNA BEDDA FACCI, QUALI AMAI

Per una bedda facci, quali amai,
fui prisu e tu cu mia cori t'accordi
iu, voluntariu, intrambu cattivai
e chiusi di catini, ferri e cordi;
o vui, ch'intrati a l'amurusi guai,
notati li mei ditti e li ricordi:
in sexxu femmininu raru, o mai,
biddizza e lealtati su concordi.

SU LI BIDDIZZI TOI TUTTI IMPERFETTI

Su li biddizzi toi tutti imperfetti
chi cu middi laidizzi allordi et ungi;
sì di sti novi e frischi citroletti
stimata fina ch'a lu culu iungi.
Sì na crapazza, pocu latti yetti,
tutta rugnusa e cui voli ti mungi;
sì troffa di zabara, hai dui sciuretti:
chi la coscia e lu pedi o feti o pungi.

THE LOVELY FACE I LOVED HAS MADE OF ME

The lovely face I loved has made of me
a prisoner and you, my heart, agreed.
I voluntarily imprisoned both of us,
with irons binding us and chains and ropes.
O you who enter the predicaments
of love, recall my words and memories:
in those of female sex it's very rare
that loyalty and beauty will concur.

ALL OF YOUR BEAUTIES ARE INDEED IMPERFECT

All of your beauties are indeed imperfect
that you make worse by adding greasy gook.
You are, it's true, esteemed down to your rump
by these young pups without experience.
But you're a shaggy sheep who gives no milk,
you're full of scabs, you're everyone's main squeeze,
you are an agave bush with two small buds:
your thighs and feet will prick or just smell bad.

DI SDEGNU E ODDIU M'È CAUSATU TANTU

Di sdegnu e oddiu m'è causatu tantu,
ch'Amuri perdi forza e lu so istintu;
costrittu su' partirmi cantu cantu
per xiri di stu 'ntricu e laberintu.
Penzandu ch'in tia amai tuttu mi spantu,
Cupidu cecu, suggiugatu e vintu:
chiù non ti ndingu né tantu, né quantu;
ora mi pari un diavolu pintu.

CU TIA FU CHIÙ DI MARI LU MIU CORI

Cu tia fu chiù di mari lu miu cori,
ch'un annu t'agghiuttiu, e be' tri simani;
e tinni, comu corpu poi chi mori,
coperti in funnu li toi modi strani:
comu cripasti lu feli 'n palori
e in atti vasci, rapaci e viddani
di giustu sdegnu unciai, ti jittai fori:
Va', e sij pastu d'auceddi e di cani.

CONTEMPT AND HATRED HAS HAD SUCH EFFECTS

Contempt and hatred have had such effects
that Love has lost its might and drive in me.
I'm forced to walk along the walls to find
the exit from these knots and labyrinth.
Blind Cupid, now in chains and vanquished,
it frightens me to think I loved you so.
No longer do you hold sway over me,
a painted devil now you seem to be.

MY HEART FOR YOU WAS GREATER THAN THE SEA

My heart for you was greater than the sea,
keeping you in me for a year, three weeks
and hiding there all your eccentric ways,
just like a body destined to die soon.
When you began to coat your words with bile,
acting in base, uncouth, rapacious ways,
I threw you out filled with complete disdain.
--Go and may birds and dogs eat your remains.

TOSTU CHI VIDI NESCIRI LA LUNA

Tostu chi vidi nesciri la luna
grida e fa malu auguriu la quagghia,
chi difittusa e varia luci duna,
ora crisci, ora è tunda ed ora squagghia.
Cu tia sdegnu mi fa quagghia importuna,
griiu chi n 'hai fermizza chi ti stagghia:
sì statua di lana, hai la persuna
vistusa in facci e l'anima di pagghia.

AMURI IN OGNI TEMPU E IN OGNI LOCU

Amuri in ogni tempu e in ogni locu
spunta supra di mia l'aurati strali
E non mi lassa mai tantu, né pocu,
Sempri risurgi egualmenti murtali.
Ridduttu su chi mi li pighiu 'n jocu.
Sàzziati, a posta tua, di lu miu mali;
Pozza crixxiri tantu lu miu focu,
perfidu Amuri, chi ti abbruxa l'ali.

THE MOMENT THE MOON RISES IN THE SKY

The moment the Moon rises in the sky
the quail begins to see it as an omen
because the planet gives a feeble light,
it grows, becomes round and then disappears.
With you, disdain makes me a vexing quail.
I yell because I see no firmness guide you;
you are a woolen statue, and your face
is lovely, but your soul's an empty space.

AT EVERY HOUR AND IN EVERY PLACE

At every hour and in every place
love blunts his golden arrows on my chest
and does not let me have a moment's rest,
ever renewing his death-dealing darts.
I've grown to take them as a kind of game.
So sate yourself at will on my harsh fate;
May the fire burning in me grow so much
deceitful love, its flames your wings to touch.

PASSAT'È LU DILLUVIU DI LI GUAI

Passat'è lu dilluviu di li guai,
siccaru l'acqui e piriu la fortuna:
Decucaliuni e Pirra divintai,
d'ogni pitruzza fazzu una pirsuna.
E di stu novu mundu, undi ristai,
gaudu vita tranquidda ed oportuna
e iettu quantu avanti disiai:
ch'amuri mi livau e sdegnu mi duna.

RUTTI SU LI CATINI E LI TINAGGHI

Rutti su li catini e li tinagghi
Li quali mi tinianu in tanti 'mbrogghi;
Passaru li stinnicchi e li badagghi
Li gilusji, rancuri e li curdogghi;
Passaru di Cupidu li battagghi:
E chiddu ch'era, mai chiù mi ci cogghi.
Pocu mi curu si m'ami e si squagghi,
Chi sdegnu m'astutau l'ardenti vogghi.

THE DELUGE OF MY WOES HAS DISAPPEARED

The deluge of my woes has disappeared,
the waters have receded and luck's vanished:
I have become Deucalion and Pyrra
and make a person out of every stone.
And in this novel world where I remain
I live a peaceful and appropriate life.
I've thrown away all that I wished before:
what love had taken, scorn did now restore.

THE PLIERS AND THE CHAINS HAVE ALL BEEN BROKEN

The pliers and the chains have all been broken
that kept me tangled up in such a mess;
the stretching and the yawning have all passed,
the jealousies, the rancors and distress;
Cupid's attacks have come and gone as well:
and what I was before, will be no more.
I care not if you love me or feel anguished,
my passion by contempt has been extinguished.

RINGRAZIU A CUI LIBBERU MI FICI

Ringraziu a cui libberu mi fici,
E adduciu l'amari mei accconiti;
Mutau lu statu riu, fatt'è filici.
Doghiusi voghi chiù non v'afflijiti:
Erivu vinti e siti vincitrici,
Libbertà, libbertà, gridati uniti;
Sdegnu xiosi, ammurtau, ruppi e disfici
lazzi, xhiammi d'amuri, strali e riti.

S'IU T'AVIA MISU IN AUTU A LU ZIMBELLU

S'iu t'avia misu in autu a lu zimbellu
fu perchì t'avvinissi zoccu avvinni:
iu l'appassiunatu e tu lu bellu,
iu puru puru e tu tutta disinni.
Sapia c'hai mancu fidi d'un ribellu,
sapia chi fraudi e no amuri ti tinni:
cussì comu a la crapa lu sturnellu
suca lu latti e siccacci li minni.

I THANK THE ONE WHO MADE ME FREE AT LAST

I thank the one who made me free at last
and turned my bitter suffering to cheer;
I'm happy now, my woeful state has passed;
painful desires, you need not suffer any more:
vanquished before, now you're victorious.
United in a voice, scream freedom, freedom.
Disdain dissolved and killed, broke and unbound
all ropes, love flames, all arrows and all bonds.

IF HIGH UPON A PEDESTAL I PLACED YOU

If high upon a pedestal I placed you
it was to let what happened come to pass:
I, as the passionate and you, the haughty one;
I, pure as snow, and you, full of deceit.
I knew you had less faith than infidels,
I knew that fraud, not love, was driving you:
just as the saying goes about the goat
how the bird sucked her milk and dried her teats.

Poichì lu focu to nun purrà chiù

Poichì lu focu to nun purrà chiù,
Chi cinniri farrà st'ossa scuntenti,
Sarò sempre custanti comu su,
E no' mi mutirà la morti a nenti.
Chi si ad un templu di Giununi fu
Cinniri ad acqua immobili, ed a venti,
Chiù gran firmizza in mia pruvirai tu,
In alma, in corpu, presenti, ed assenti.

Di nuddu tempu la mia faccia è asciutta

Di nuddu tempu la mia faccia è asciutta
Né di li celi 'mpetru mai faguri;
Beata tia, Aretusa, chi riddutta
A trasformarti in lu to propiu omuri,
Fuiendu Alfeu per sutterranea grutta
D'Elide vai 'n Sicilia tutti l'huri:
Cuss'iu ci jissi supra terra o sutta
Squagghiatu in sangu, in lagrimi o in suduri.

WHEN YOUR FIRE CAN NO LONGER FEED ON ME

When your fire can no longer feed on me,
for it will have reduced my sorry bones
to ashes, ever constant I will be,
for even death cannot affect my love.
For if the temple of great Juno was
ashes resistant to both wind and water,
you'll find in me much greater constancy,
as soul or body, here or absently.

THERE'S NOT A DAY WHEN MY FACE IS TEARS FREE

There's not a day when my face is tears free,
nor favors ever do I beg from heaven;
O blessèd Arethusa, who to flee
Alpheus,* changed yourself into a stream
and flowed from distant Greece to Sicily,
along a deep and subterranean cave,
if only I could go there, underground or not,
even transformed in blood, in tears or sweat.

* Note: the poet is referring to the myth of Arethusa who in order to flee the amorous
intentions of Alpheus was changed into a river that flows through underground caves
beneath the Aegean sea and emerges in Siracusa. But Alpheus was also changed into a
stream to join his beloved. The poet is expressing his desire to return to Sicily from his
captivity from his Algerian prison.

Poi chi ti mustri sdignusa ed autera
Contra di cui ti brama e ti disia,
O facci d'una perfida chimera,
Aspettu d'una iniqua e fera Arpia;
Fazzuni smostri e quali a na pantera
Ed in effettu tigri e Idra ria:
Di poi ch'è fatta la mundana sfera
Mai non fu parsa chiù laida di tia.

Since you display such haughtiness and scorn
against a man who yearns and burns for you,
you're nothing but a fraudulent illusion.
Your face is like a Harpy, mean and fierce,
a real monstrosity just like a panther,
nay a real tiger, and a fearsome hydra:
from the beginning of the universe
there's never been a woman more perverse.

Proverbii

Proverbs

TINTU CUI SERVI AD UN PATRUNI INGRATU

Tintu cui servi ad un patruni ingratu
cecu cui campa sempri irrisolutu
guai pri cui lassa chiddu chi c'è datu,
stultu chi cerca risposta d'un mutu
infami cui a lu mali sta ostinatu,
misiru cui nun ha riparu o scutu,
scuntenti cui d'amuri è travagghiatu,
tintu cui cadi pri chiamari ajutu.

VIDI E TACI SI BENI AVIRI VOI

Vidi e taci si beni aviri voi,
la cosa nu la diri si nun sai,
vogghini cchiù pri li vicini toi
chi non pri cui nu lu vidisti mai,
ama l'amicu cu li vizij soi,
porta rispettu a locu undi stai,
nun fari cchiù di chiddu chi tu poi,
pensa la cosa innanti chi la fai.

PITY THE MAN WHO SERVES UNGRATEFUL MASTERS

Pity the man who serves ungrateful masters;
blind is the man who lives without resolve;
woe to the man who leaves what's given him;
fools are those who want answers from a mute;
wretched the man who clings to evildoing;
wretched's the man who has no shield or refuge;
unhappy is the man whom love travails;
pity the man who falls while help he hails.

SEE AND BE QUIET IF YOU WANT GOOD THINGS

See and be quiet if you want good things;
don't say a word if you don't know the facts;
always support the folks who are your neighbors,
rather than those you've never seen before;
and love your friend together with his faults;
respect the place where you have made your home;
do not attempt to do more than you can;
before you do a thing, have a good plan.

A POCU PANI LU CORPU T'INSIGNA

A pocu pani lu corpu t'insigna:
cui fa cussì la spisa si sparagna;
cui voli focu assai porti assai ligna,
cui voli robba assai vaja in Cuccagna.
Lu megghiu è stari sulu a la tua vigna,
chi, cui sta sulu, di nuddu si lagna,
lu muttu anticu lu modu m'insigna:
cui joca sulu sulu mai s'incagna.

LA FERLA È LA PAGURA DI LA SCOLA

La ferla è la pagura di la scola,
la casa nun s'acchiana senza scala,
d' Amuri nasci amuri, mentri vola,
la furca è fatta pri la genti mala,
la tila nun si tessi senza spola,
lu tronu li cosi auti rumpi e scala,
l'acqua leva la rugia e no la mola,
pagura guarda vigna e non sipala

Having Little Bread to Eat Teaches Your Body

Having no bread to eat will teach your body;
this way you will save on the food you need,
if you want a big fire, bring lots of wood,
if you want lots of land, go to Cockaigne.
It's best to live alone in your own vineyard,
for he who lives alone does not complain.
The ancient saying teaches us the way:
in order to get angry two must play.

The Stick Creates the Fear in a Schoolhouse

The stick creates the fear in a schoolhouse;
you cannot build a house without a ladder;
Love fosters love while it is flying high;
the gallows are created for bad folks;
you cannot weave a cloth without a spool;
thunder breaks all high things and lowers them;
water removes rust, not the grinding wheel;
no cactus blade will guard your vines, fear will.

A BON PILOTU NUN MANCA VASCEDDU

A bon pilotu nun manca vasceddu,
a bon vasceddu nun manca timuni,
a bon suldatu nun manca casteddu,
a bon casteddu megghiu turriuni,
a cavaleri un bon cavaddu beddu,
a lu cavaddu la virga e spiruni,
ad un bon nidu nun manca auceddu,
ed a bon scavu nun manca patruni.

PRI TROPPU VENTU LA VASCEDDU SFERRA

Pri troppu ventu la vasceddu sferra,
e pri gran frevi lu malatu sparra,
pi assai cunsigghi si perdi la guerra,
e pri tanti giudizii si sgarra.
Lauda la mari e teniti a la terra,
pensa la cosa innanti chi si parra,
pirch'aju 'ntisu diri a la mia terra:
cui fa li cosi adaxiu, ma li sgarra.

A WORTHY PILOT DOES NOT LACK A SHIP

A worthy pilot does not lack a ship;
a worthy ship a rudder does not lack;
a worthy soldier does not lack a castle;
a worthy castle has a better tower;
a knight deserves a handsome steed;
a horse requires both a stick and spurs;
a worthy nest does not lack for a bird;
and a good slave does not lack for a lord.

THE SHIP WILL FOUNDER WHEN THERE'S TOO MUCH WIND

The ship will founder when there's too much wind;
and with high fever the sick man will ramble;
a war's lost when too many voices speak;
and for too much advice mistakes are made.
Give praises to the sea, but stay on land;
think well before you start to speak your mind,
for I have heard it said around my way
that those who do things slowly never stray.

TUTTI LI COSI VANNU A LU PINDINU

Tutti li cosi vannu a lu pindinu,
ed a lu peju si c'inclina ogn'unu;
a cui leva a cui duna lu distinu,
e nun ci pari mai lu nostru dunu.
Nun curri paru lu nostru caminu,
pocu cridi lu saggiu a l'importunu;
lu riccu mancu cridi a lu mischinu,
lu saturu nun cridi a lu dijunu.

CUI CANCIA LA VIA VECCHIA PRI LA NOVA

Cui cancia la via vecchia pri la nova
chiddu chi mancu si penza ci avveni;
non vaja scausa cui simina chiova,
chi poi si pungi cu duluri e peni;
cui va a l'abissu a l'abissu si trova,
cui simina virtù ricoghi beni,
e ben l'antichi ndi ficiru prova:
cui sputa in celu a la facci ci veni.

EVERYTHING NOW IS GOING DOWNHILL IT SEEMS

Every thing now is running down the slope,
and everyone leans toward the worst of things.
Destiny takes from some and gives to others,
and we don't seem to think ours is a gift.
Our journey does not run quite evenly;
The wise man pays no mind to vexing folk;
The wealthy don't believe folks hungering;
those sated don't believe in dieting.

HE WHO WILL CHANGE THE OLD FOR SOMETHING NEW

He who will change the old for something new,
will see things happen he did not foresee;
Let her who sows nails not walk without shoes,
for she will then be stuck with pains and woes;
He who seeks hell will find himself in hell;
He who sows virtue will then goodness reap;
The ancient folks the proof of this knew well:
if you spit high, on your face spit will fall.

SU STATU AMICU SENZA MENDA O TACCA

Su statu amicu senza menda o tacca,
fermu cchiù assai di scoghiu o forti rocca,
ed ogni amicu mi sciogghi ed attacca
e sonu a chidda parti undi mi tocca;
e si cu mia l'amuri forsi stracca
e si dimustra di natura sciocca,
cui chiù pò fari fa, cui ammacca ammacca,
la varca undi va va, zara a cui tocca.

L'OMU A LU MUNDU PRI SO CONSUETU

L'omu a lu mundu pri so consuetu
è di middi pinzeri travagghiatu,
anzi si cridi sempri stari inquietu
perchì sulu a l'affanni è destinatu;
megghiu è lu pocu e guadiri quietu,
chi l'assai pussidiri in malu statu,
talchì a lu mundu pri campari letu,
megghiu è sulu chi malu accumpagnatu.

I'VE BEEN A FRIEND WITHOUT A FAULT OR FLAW

I've been a friend without a fault or flaw,
faithful and firmer than a rock or fortress,
and every friend I have unties and binds me
and I feel every blow that lands on me.
and so if love perhaps has waned a bit,
showing itself to have a foolish nature,
let all do what they will, let the blows rain,
the boat goes where it wills, may the best win.

.

IN GENERAL MAN ON THIS EARTH IS PREY

In general man on this earth is prey
to harsh travails of many varied kinds.
In fact, he thinks he's always restless
because his destiny is full of woes;
It's better to have little and live quietly
than having great possessions and be sad,
so that in this world to live happily,
better to be alone than in bad company.

CHIDDU È LU BON'AMICU, CHI TI DICI

Chiddu è lu bon'amicu, chi ti dici
lu bellu è guasta la cosa mendaci;
chiddu è lu megghiu fruttu, chi si fici,
chidda è la bona, chi vidi e chi taci,
chiddu è l'arberu bonu, ch'ha radici,
chiddu è valenti, chi cumbatti audaci,
chiddu è lu riccu, chi campa filici,
chidd' è la bedda, ch'a lu cori piaci.

DUMANDU AJUTU A LU MIU CHIANTU AMARU

Dumandu ajutu a lu miu chiantu amaru
a cui mi teni pri crudu e ribeddu,
e mentri penzu farici riparu
chiù mi junci cuteddu a lu cuteddu;
sugnu custrittu stari a lu succaru,
sugnu custrittu jiri a lu maceddu:
pirchì mi pari gatta di firraru,
chi s'addurmenta a sonu di marteddu.

GOOD IS THE FRIEND WHO TELLS YOU WHAT IS GOOD

Good is the friend who tells you what is good
and speaks against mendacious facts and deeds;
best is the fruit that is allowed to ripen;
good is the maid who sees and does not speak;
good is the tree whose roots are very deep;
courageous is the man who fights with daring;
wealthy's the man who lives without a care;
the girl who pleases you, she's the most fair.

I CALL FOR HELP AGAINST MY BITTER TEARS

I call for help against my bitter tears
to the mean one who holds me cruelly,
and while I think I've found a way to flee,
she catches me with yet another knife.
I am, therefore, constrained, strapped to the ropes,
and to the slaughterhouse I'm forced to go:
therefore to me she's like the blacksmith's cat
who sleeps through hammering no matter what.

Ogni pocu faidda fa gran focu,
ed ogni focu fa fari gran xiamma;
ogni picciulu amuri fattu a jocu
in qualchi sorti ed in qualch'ura inxiamma;
servi l'amicu, servi a tempu e a locu,
ed ogni poca forza scippa, smamma;
ogni virmuzzu smangia qualchi pocu,
ogni pitrudda servi a la maramma.

RESISTI A LA FORTUNA ED A LI TORTI

Resisti a la fortuna ed a li torti,
e campa comu poi cu ingegnu ed arti;
s'hai bona sorti tenitila forti,
e canta si ti cantanu li carti;
supporta chiddu pisu chi tu porti,
e sii primu a pigghiari si si sparti;
nun t'incagnari mai cu la tua sorti,
chi, cui s'incagna, perdi la sua parti.

A LITTLE SPARK BEGETS A GREAT GREAT FIRE

A little spark begets a great, great fire
and every fire will generate high flames.
Each little love that starts as in a game
will burst into a flame sometime, somehow.
At the right time and place, a friend is useful,
and every little effort chips away.
Every small worm will form a little hole,
and every little stone adds to the whole.

RESIST AGAINST BAD FORTUNE AND OFFENSES

Resist against bad fortune and offenses,
and live as well you can with art and wit.
If you've good luck, hold on to it with care,
and sing if your cards sing a tune you like.
Endure the burden that is yours to bear
and be the first to take more if it lessens.
Don't ever get distressed about your lot,
for those who get distressed will lose the pot.